JR. GRAPHIC AMERICAN LEGENDS

# PAUL BUNYAN

Andrea P. Smith

PowerKiDS press

New York

Published in 2012 by The Rosen Publishing Group, Inc.
29 East 21st Street, New York, NY 10010

First Edition

Editor: Joanne Randolph
Book Design: Planman Technologies
Illustrations: Planman Technologies

Library of Congress Cataloging-in-Publication Data

Smith, Andrea P.
Paul Bunyan / by Andrea P. Smith. — 1st ed.
      p. cm. — (Jr. graphic American legends)
Summary: Relates in graphic novel format some of the exploits of Paul Bunyan, a lumberjack said to be taller than the trees whose pet was a blue ox named Babe. Includes index.
ISBN 978-1-4488-5191-1 (library binding) — ISBN 978-1-4488-5220-8 (pbk.) — ISBN 978-1-4488-5221-5 (6-pack)
1. Bunyan, Paul (Legendary character)—Legends. 2. Bunyan, Paul (Legendary character)—Comic books, strips, etc. 3. Graphic novels. [1. Graphic novels. 2. Bunyan, Paul (Legendary character)—Legends. 3. Folklore—United States. 4. Tall tales.] I. Title.
PZ7.7.S558Pau 2012
398.2—dc22
[E]

2011001836

Manufactured in the United States of America

CPSIA Compliance Information: Batch #PLS1102PK: For Further Information contact Rosen Publishing, New York, New York at 1-800-237-9932

# Contents

# Main Characters

Paul Bunyan An American Legend. According to folklore, Paul Bunyan was a giant lumberjack who worked in the northern forests of the United States and Canada.

Paul Bonjean A French-Canadian logger. He fought against the British in the Papineau **Rebellion**. This rebellion was fought in an effort to keep upper and lower Canada from uniting.

Big Joe Montferrand (1802–1864) Famous Canadian logger. He ran a logging camp.

Fabian "Saginaw Joe" Fournier (1845–1875) A French-Canadian logger. He worked for the H.M. Loud Company.

James MacGillivray A newspaper reporter. He wrote the first collection of stories about Paul Bunyan.

William Laughead (1882–1958) Advertising manager for the Red River Lumber Company. He wrote several **pamphlets** about Paul Bunyan.

# PAUL BUNYAN

IN THE 1800S, LOGGERS CUT DOWN TREES IN CANADA AND THE UNITED STATES.

8

ONE WINTER, BLUE SNOW FELL FROM THE SKY.

WHAT HAVE WE GOT HERE? IT'S A BABY OX.

MOO! Moo!

I'LL NAME YOU BABE, THE BLUE OX.

PAUL KEPT BABE AND GAVE HIM A BARN TO SLEEP IN.

WHEN WE GOT UP THIS MORNING, BABE WAS GONE. AND SO WAS HIS BARN!

HE WANDERED INTO THIS FIELD.

WHO WAS THE REAL PAUL BUNYAN, THOUGH? HE MIGHT HAVE BEEN A MAN NAMED PAUL BONJEAN.

IN 1837, PAUL BONJEAN LED CANADIAN LOGGERS INTO BATTLE AGAINST THE BRITISH.

JOE RAN A LOGGING CAMP IN CANADA.

YOUR MEN ARE TOO SLOW.

THEY'RE WORKING AS FAST AS THEY CAN. NOW GET OUT OF MY CAMP!

DID YOU SEE THAT?

LOOK HOW BIG JOE STOOD UP FOR US!

IN ADDITION TO LOGGING, JOE GOT A **REPUTATION** FOR FIGHTING.

AFTER JOE DIED IN 1875, HIS **EXPLOITS** BECAME LEGENDARY.

JOE COULD BEAT ANYONE IN A FIGHT.

DID YOU EVER SEE HIM EAT BARK OFF A TREE?

I HEARD HE HAD TWO SETS OF TEETH.

WHEN I WAS YOUNG, I WORKED FOR A LOGGING COMPANY. YOU WOULDN'T BELIEVE WHAT I HEARD.

WRITE IT DOWN. WE'LL PUT IT IN OUR PAPER.

I'LL CALL MY STORY "THE ROUND RIVER DRIVE."

IT'S A STORY ABOUT A MAN NAMED PAUL BUNYAN!

LET ME SEE, LET ME SEE!

ABOUT THE SAME TIME, WILLIAM LAUGHEAD WROTE DOWN SOME STORIES THAT HE'D HEARD FROM AN OLD LOGGER.

HAVE YOU HEARD THE STORY ABOUT PAUL AND THE ROUND RIVER?

NO, TELL ME ABOUT IT.

THE REDRIVER LUMBER COMPANY

THESE STORIES ABOUT PAUL BUNYAN ARE GREAT.

YOU CAN USE THEM TO **ADVERTISE** YOUR LUMBER.

SOON EVERYONE IN THE COUNTRY KNEW ABOUT PAUL BUNYAN AND BABE.

PAUL BUNYAN

CALIFORNIA PINE

FROM

THE RED RIVER

LUMBER COMPANY

# Timeline

| | |
|---|---|
| **1607** | Logging begins in America when the Jamestown settlers cut down trees to build houses. |
| **1820s** | The first sawmill was built in the Pacific Northwest. |
| **1830s** | Bangor, Maine becomes the largest supplier of lumber around the world. |
| **1837** | Paul Bonjean fights in the Papineau Rebellion in which French-Canadians revolt against the British. |
| **Mid 1800s** | Paper mills begin making paper from wood pulp instead of other materials, such as rags. |
| **1862** | The Homestead Act gives settlers 160 acres (65 ha) of land west of the Mississippi River. The land is heavily wooded and needs to be cleared of trees. |
| **1865–1875** | Fabian "Saginaw Joe" Fournier works for the H. M. Loud Company. |
| **1905** | The state of Washington produces more lumber than anywhere else in America. |
| **1910** | James MacGillivray's collection of Paul Bunyan stories, called "The Round River Drive," is printed in a Detroit newspaper. |
| **1916** | William Laughead writes about Paul Bunyan as part of an advertising campaign for the Red River Lumber Company. |
| **1922** | The Red River Company publishes *The Marvelous Exploits of Paul Bunyan*. This book brings widespread attention to the legend. |
| **1996** | The U. S. Post Office issues a Paul Bunyan stamp. |

# Glossary

**advertise** (AD-vur-tyz)  To announce publicly, often to try to sell something.

**cradle** (KRAY-dul)  A baby's small bed.

**exploit** (EK-sployt) )  An adventure.

**feller** (FEL-er)  A man or a boy; it comes from the word *fellow*. It also was used to talk about loggers, who felled trees.

**legend** (LEH-jend)  A story, passed down through the years, that cannot be proved.

**logger** (LOG-er)  A person who cuts down trees as a job.

**pamphlet** (PAM-flit)  Unbound papers that are published either with no cover or with a paper cover.

**porridge** (POR-ij)  Grain boiled with water until thick and soft, like oatmeal.

**rebellion** (rih-BEL-yun)  A fight against one's government.

**reputation** (reh-pyoo-TAY-shun)  The ideas people have about another person, an animal, or an object.

**statue** (STA-chyoo)  An image of a person or an animal, usually cut in clay, metal, or stone.

**tale** (TAYL)  A story.

**timber** (TIM-ber)  A warning called out to tell loggers that a cut tree is falling.

# Index

# Web Sites

Due to the changing nature of Internet links, Power Kids Press has developed an online list of Web sites related to the subject of this book. This site is updated regularly. Please use this link to access the list:

www.powerkidslinks.com/JGAM/bunyan